Boys

Sticker Activity Book

priddy books
big ideas for little people

This book belongs to

..... Caidyn Gribben ....

Terry's toolbox

Can you find the stickers to give Terry some tools?

Ben the builder

Find the stickers to give Ben a smiley face!

Hammer time

How many blue hammers can you count?

Super skyscraper

Colour in the skyscraper.

How many floors are there?

Build a house

Can you find the stickers to help build this house?

Matching mates

Can you draw lines between the matching builders?

Builder's yard

Find the stickers to show which trucks
are parked in the builder's yard.

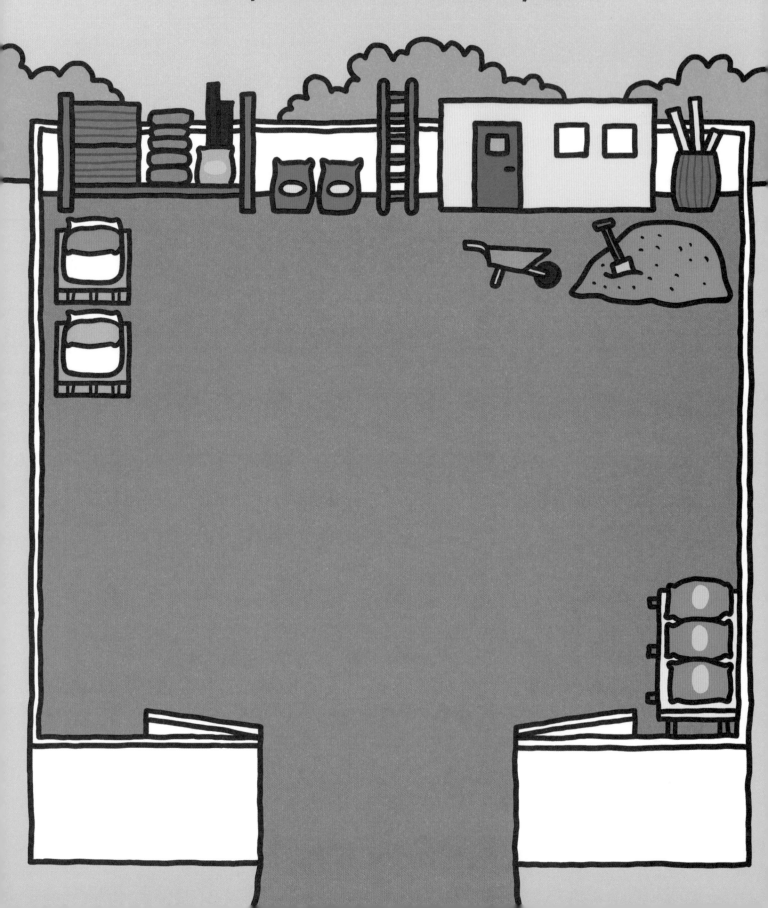

Learn to draw

Can you copy this picture of a bulldozer?

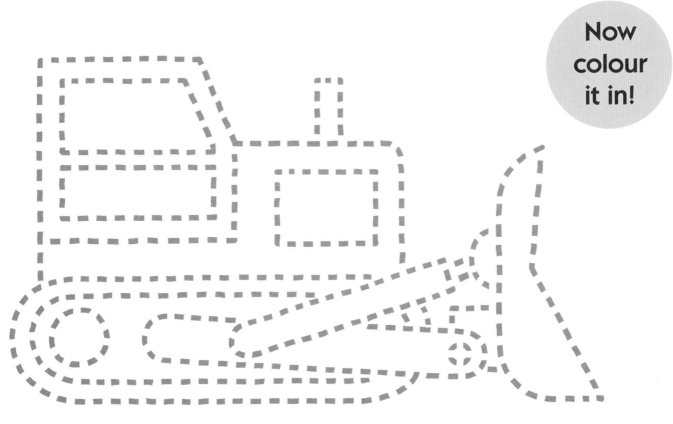

Now colour it in!

At the building site

Find the stickers to show who's working
at the building site today.

Can you spot the purple bucket?

Freddy Forklift

Colour in the forklift truck.

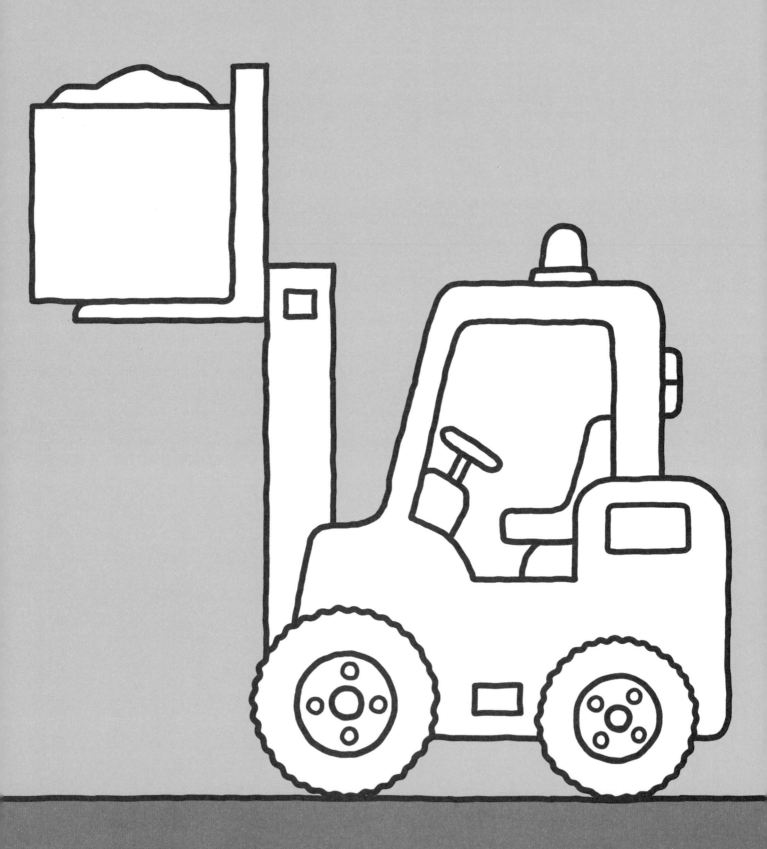

Odd one out

Which one of the builders has lost his hardhat?

Plumbing maze

Follow the pipes to help the mouse escape!

Barry's truck

Find the stickers to fill the builder's truck.

What colour is Barry's truck?

Building in the city

How many builders can you count?

Now colour in the crane!

Missing nails

Can you find the stickers to give the builders their nails?

Dot-to-dot

Join the dots to complete this picture of a giant excavator.

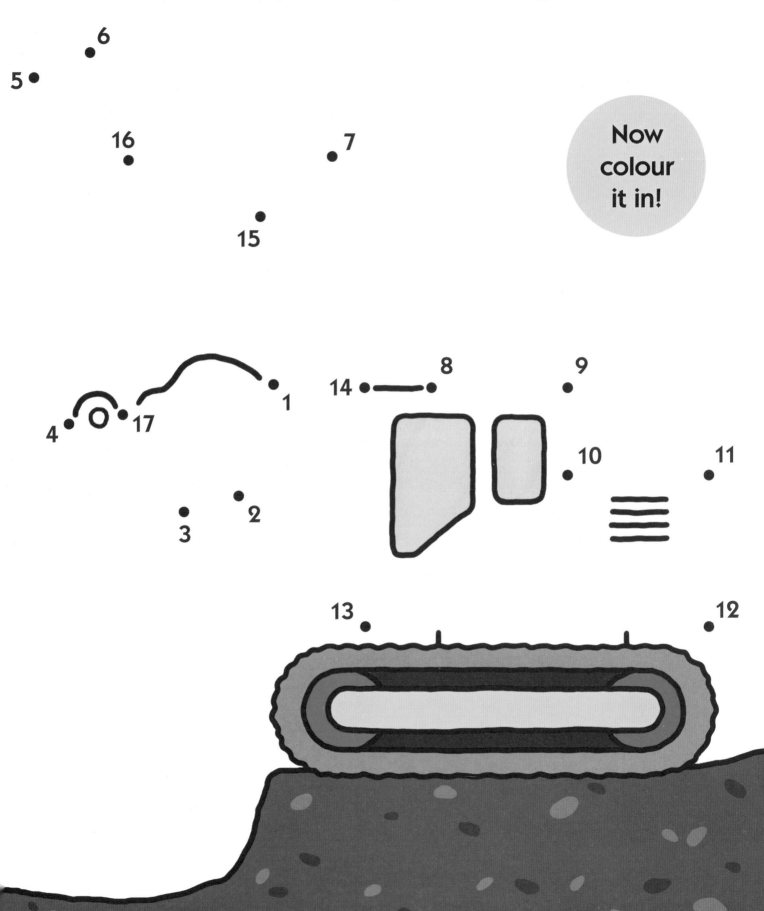

Now colour it in!

Toolbox trail

Follow the trail to help Trevor get to his toolbox.

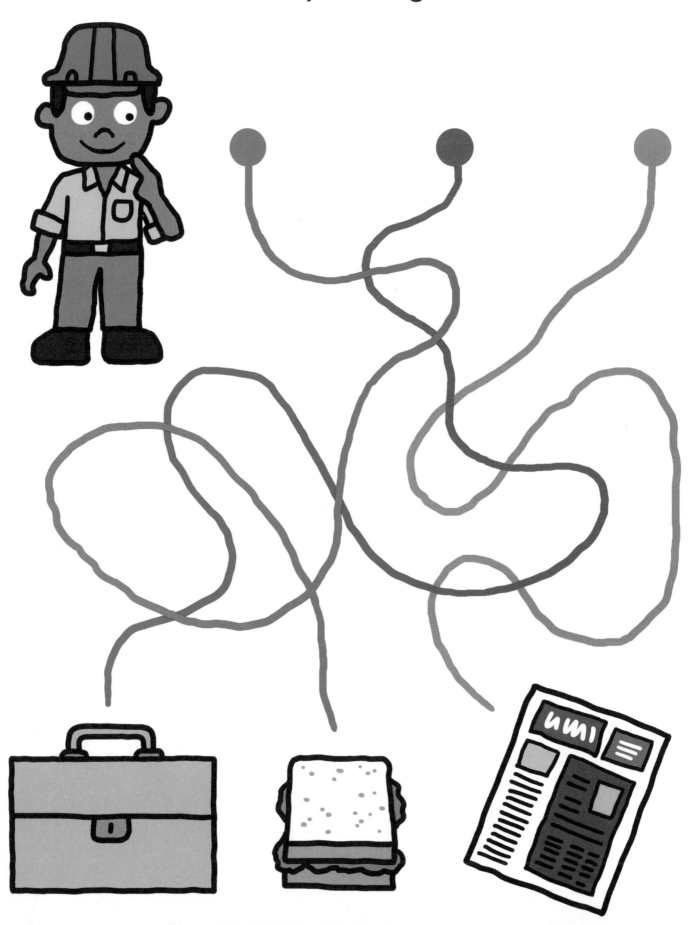

Hilda the builder

Find the stickers to give Hilda a smiley face!

Match and make

Match the builders with their materials!

Saw

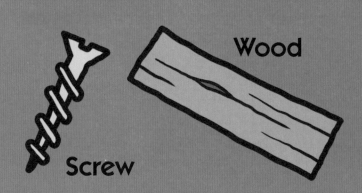

Screwdriver

Cement

Nail

Wood

Screw

Trowel

Hammer

Dump trucks

How many yellow dump trucks can you count?

Construction city

Find the stickers to decorate the city.

Can you colour in the park?

Learn to draw

Can you copy this picture of a crane?

Now colour it in!

Scary scaffolding

Find the stickers to make this scaffolding safe!

Busy builders

Can you colour in this crowded building site?

Spot the difference

Can you spot the five differences between the two builder's bags?

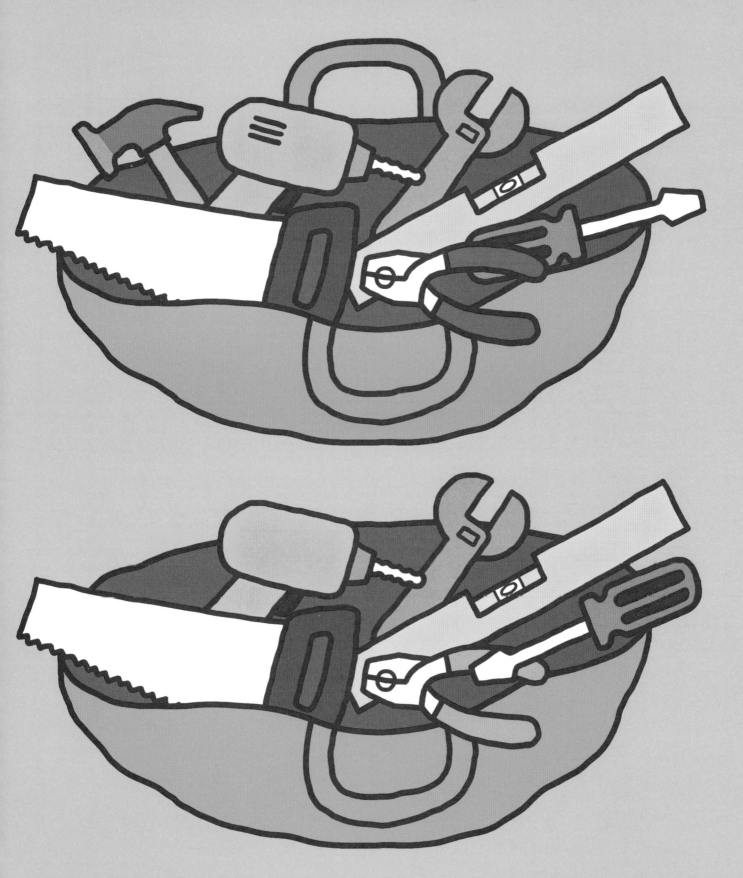

Missing tools

Can you find the stickers of these builders' tools?

Ship's deck

Find the stickers to decorate the deck.

Escape trail

Help the pirate ship find the right trail to get to the safety of the desert island!

Jungle fun

Colour in the Treasure Island jungle scene.

Pete the pirate

Find the stickers to give Pete a smiley face.

Learn to draw

Can you copy this picture of a cannon?

Now colour it in!

What's missing?

Which pirate is missing his cutlass?

Count the compasses

How many compasses can you count?

Under the sea

Find the stickers to decorate the seabed.

Desert Island

Find the stickers to decorate the pirate's island.

Where is the treasure buried?

Treasure maze

Help Jolly Roger find the treasure!

Monkey mischief

Which monkey has stolen the captain's telescope?

Pirate pub

How many bottles can you count?

Walk the plank

Add the scary shark stickers to the sea.

Counting hats

How many captain hats can you count?

Captain Catherine

Can you colour in the pirate captain?

X marks the spot

Find the stickers to put on this treasure map.

Can you find the X sticker?

I spy

Colour in the pirate's telescope.

Setting sail

This ship is missing its flag, anchor and cannon.
Can you find the right stickers?

Dot-to-dot

Join the dots to complete this picture
of a skull and crossbones.

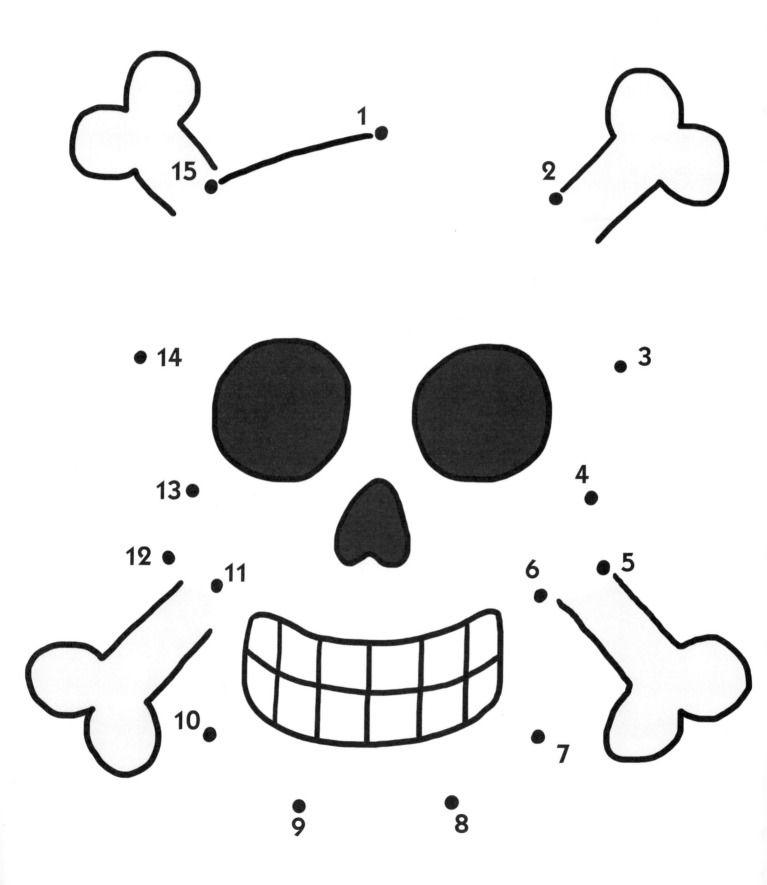

Matching ships

Can you draw a line to match the pirates with their ships?

Pip the pirate

Find the stickers to give Pip a smiley face.

Pirate trail

Give Captain Charlie a hand and follow
the trail to find his missing hook.

Secret cave

Find the stickers to decorate the pirate cave.

Where will you put the bat stickers?

Treasure trouble

Which treasure chest has a nasty surprise inside it?

Learn to draw

Can you copy this picture of a crocodile?

Now colour him in!

Palm pirates

Can you find the coconut stickers to put on the tree?

Pretty Pollys

Can you spot the five differences between the two parrots?

Captain club

These pirates are missing their captain hats.
Can you find the right stickers?

Can you give them names?

Dinosaur
Sticker
Activity
Fun

Big and small

Dinosaurs could be very big or very small,
find the stickers to complete the chart.

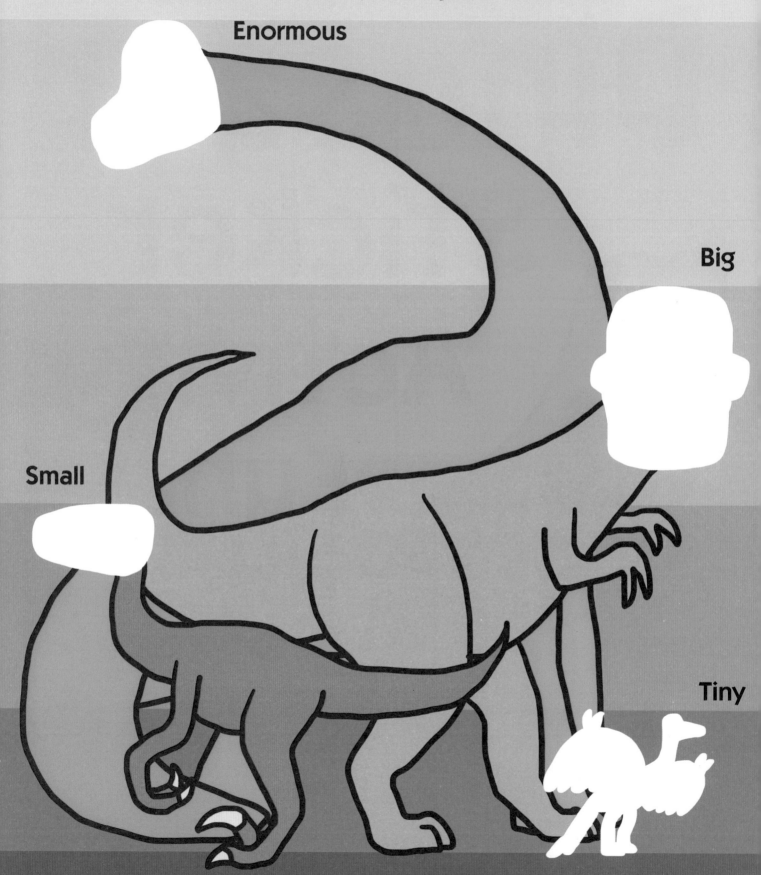

Enormous

Big

Small

Tiny

Dino trail

Help this mummy to her nest of babies!

Odd one out

Which dinosaur likes eating other dinosaurs?

Dinosaur faces

Can you give this T. Rex a scary face?

Dino bones

How many dinosaur bones can you count?

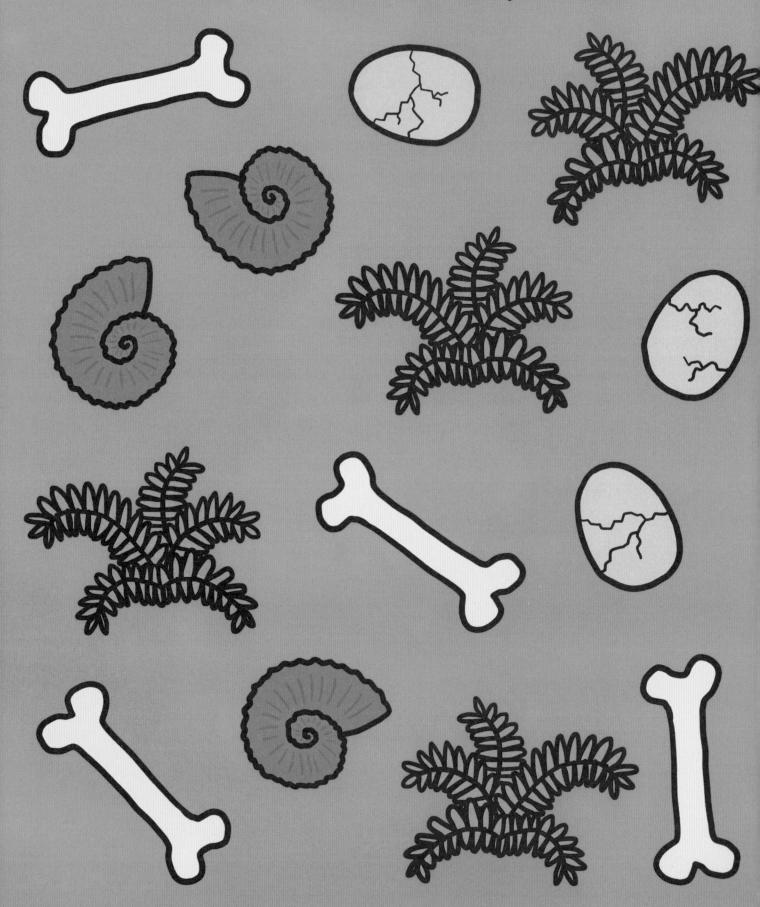

Dino jungle

Colour in this jungle full of dinosaurs.

Flying reptiles

Find the stickers to decorate this flying reptiles scene.

Matching friends

Can you draw lines between the matching dinosaurs?

Skeleton sketch

Find the missing bone stickers to complete the picture.

Learn to draw

Can you copy this picture of a Triceratops?

Now colour it in.

Under the sea

Find the stickers to show who's under the sea.

Colour in the seaweed.

Speedy dinosaurs

Colour in the Velociraptors.

Stripes and spots

Can you spot the spotty dinosaur?

Who has horns on his head?

Dino maze

Help this baby dinosaur find his mum!

Hide and seek

Find the stickers to show who's hiding in the dinosaur cave.

Fossils in the forest

How many fossils can you count in the prehistoric forest?

Colour in the dinosaur.

Family day out

Who's walking behind mummy dinosaur?

Scary T. Rex

Join the dots to complete this picture of T. Rex.

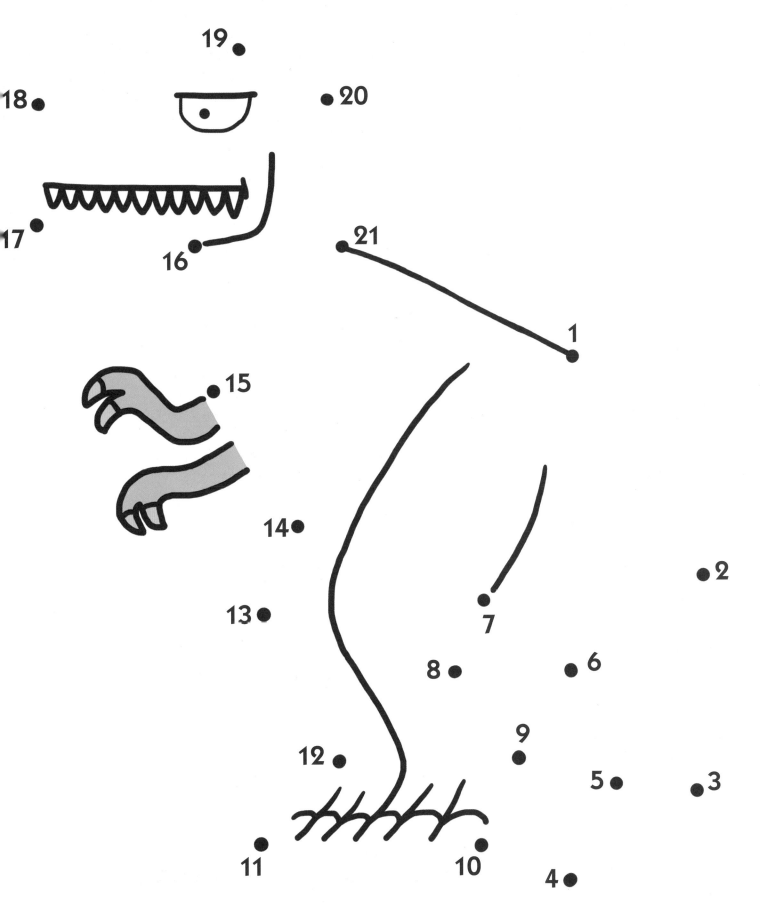

Rex's trail

Help Rex find the right trail to get to his bone!

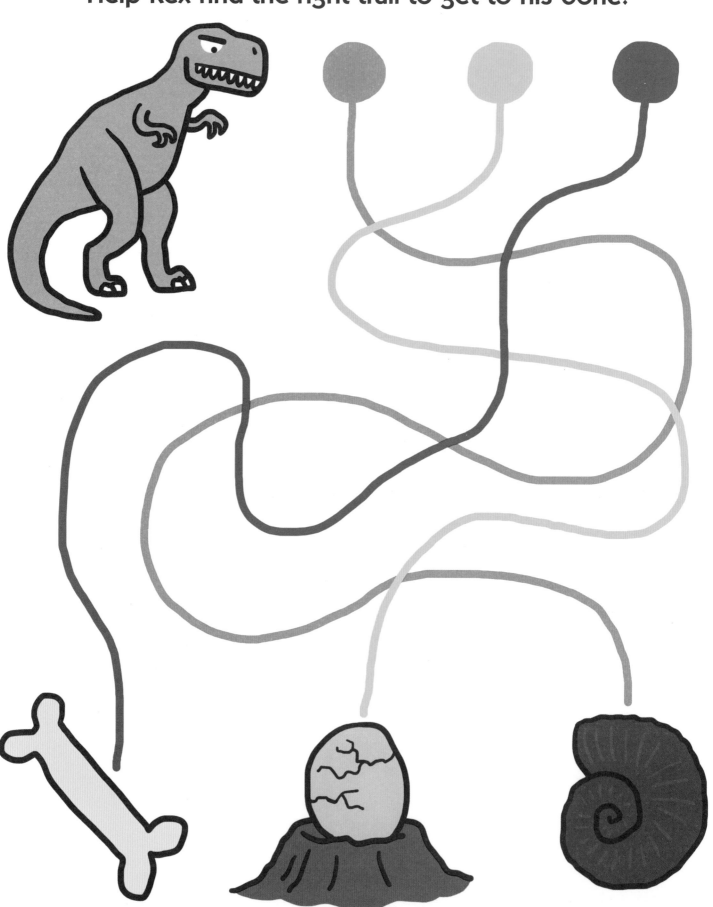

Colourful counting

How many blue dinosaurs can you see?

Happy families

Can you match the mummies with their babies?

Dinosaur faces

Can you give Tommy Triceratops a smiley face?

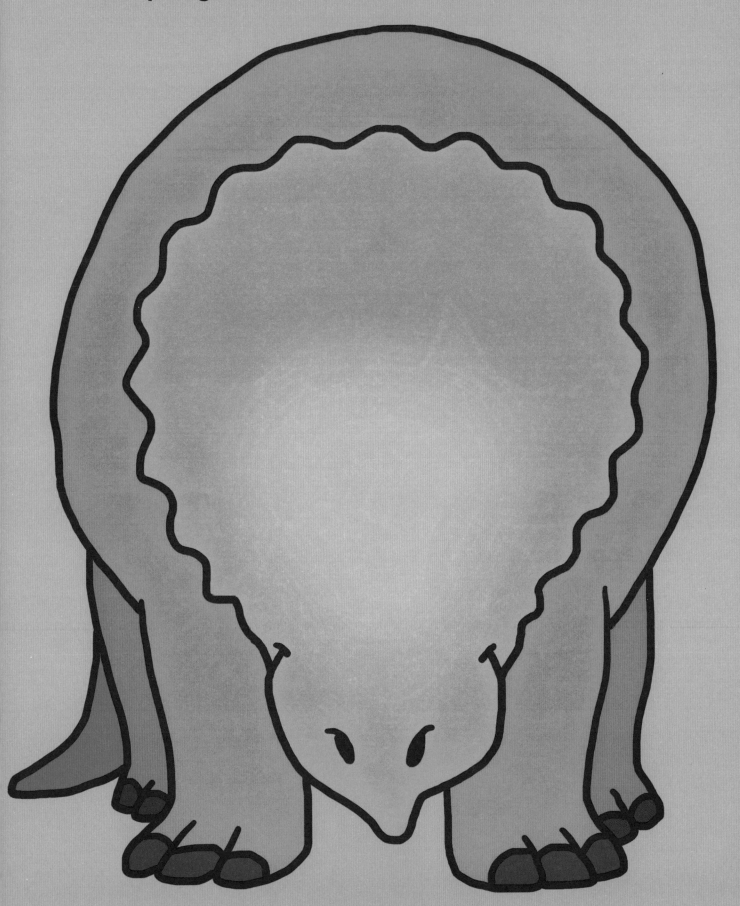

Prehistoric land

Find the stickers to show which dinosaurs
are roaming the prehistoric land.

Learn to draw

Trace the dotted line to draw the Pterosaur.

Now colour it in!

Susie Stegosaurus

Can you find the stickers to give Susie her missing spikes?

Gentle giant

Colour in the huge Brachiosaurus.

Different dinos

Can you spot the five differences between these two bone-headed dinosaurs?

Volcano

Which dino friends are playing by the volcano?